The Steam Engine

GREAT INVENTIONS

The Steam Engine

JAMES LINCOLN COLLIER

Marshall Cavendish
Benchmark
New York

Marshall Cavendish Benchmark
99 White Plains Road
Tarrytown, NY 10591-9001
www.marshallcavendish.us

Library of Congress Cataloging-in-Publication Data

Collier, James Lincoln, 1928–
The steam engine / by James Lincoln Collier.
p. cm. — (Great inventions)
Summary: "Follows the development of the steam engine"—Provided by publisher.
Includes bibliographical references and index.
ISBN 0-7614-1880-6
1. Steam-engines—Juvenile literature. I. Title. II. Series.
TJ467.C55 2005
621.1—dc22
200402181

Series design by Sonia Chaghatzbanian

Photo research by Candlepants Incorporated

Cover photo: The Image Works/Public Records Office/Topham-HIP

The photographs in this book are used by permission and through the courtesy of: *Getty Images:*
Central Press/Stringer, 2; Hulton Archive, 8, 34, 37, 54, 56, 63, 65, 78, 80, 89; Time Life Pictures,
92. *The Image Works:* Science Museum, London/Topham-HIP, 11, 14, 16, 18, 24, 28, 32, 38, 42, 46,
52; Topham, 20, 30, 68; ARPL/Topham, 23, 36; Ann Ronan Picture Library/HIP, 26, 94-95; NRM,
York/Topham-HIP, 48, 51, 58. *Corbis:* 60, 71, 72, 75; Bettmann, 13, 44, 83, 86; Museum of the City
of New York, 40; Gianni Dagli Orti, 66; Underwood and Underwood, 85; Lester Lefkowitz, 90.

Printed in China

1 3 5 6 4 2

CONTENTS

The Steam Engine

THIS NINETEENTH-CENTURY PORTABLE STEAM ENGINE COULD BE BROUGHT TO A FARM OR INTO A FIELD TO RUN AGRICULTURAL MACHINERY. THE LARGE PULLEYS ON EITHER SIDE OF THE FUNNEL-SHAPED SMOKE-STACK WERE ATTACHED TO SIMILAR PULLEYS ON THE MACHINE THAT NEEDED TO BE POWERED.

Power for the Machine Age

In an age when our world is powered by electricity and oil, we little remember the importance of steam in creating the great industrial system. The steam engine was one of the most important inventions ever. Had it not been devised when it was, our world would be much different.

Today almost everybody believes that this great system of power was invented by James Watt. His name is always on everybody's list of great inventors, along with Thomas Alva Edison, Michael Faraday, and the Wright brothers. Yet the steam engine was not invented by Watt, but by an Englishman named Thomas Newcomen almost twenty-five years before Watt was born.

Why was Newcomen largely forgotten? There was only one brief mention of his death in the press, and we are not even sure where he is buried. This lack of attention was, in part, due to the fact that Newcomen was a practical man of business, mainly interested in finding ways to do things better. At the time—and even today—honors and prestige went to the people who searched out theories and principles, like Isaac Newton, who worked out the principles of gravity, or Albert Einstein, who developed the theory of relativity. For example, it was fifty years after Hans Christian Oersted and Faraday separately worked out the principle of the electric motor that anyone figured out how to make one. Yet the work of Faraday and Oersted is thoroughly discussed in physics textbooks, while the name of the man who built the first electric motor is today forgotten. Newcomen was not an intellectual, not someone interested in big ideas but in simply making something work. The intellectuals tended to look down their noses at him.

A second problem was that a man named Thomas Savery had built a few steam engines before Newcomen. Savery's machines were largely ineffective, able to pump enough water for the fountains in rich people's gardens, but no use for much else. Savery, however, was good at publicizing himself, and, until recently, accounts of the development of the steam engine often put his name ahead of Newcomen's.

In the twentieth century, Newcomen's role in shaping the modern world has increasingly been recognized. One historian says that Newcomen was "the first great mechanical engineer, and his successful creation was of incalculable importance . . . for the world." Yet even today, as we approach the three hundredth anniversary of his invention, students are more likely to hear about James Watt's accomplishments than his.

There is no question that Newcomen's invention was of incalculable importance. The period beginning in the late 1500s in Europe and continuing to today saw a burst of invention and scientific discovery far beyond anything that had happened in the entire history of humankind previously. One result of this dazzling inventive explosion was the Industrial Revolution, which began in Europe, especially England, in about 1760, continued in the United States in the early 1800s, and is still occurring in the developing nations.

The Industrial Revolution transformed human life. Before it took place, most human beings—probably 90 percent of them—were farmers, the largest proportion of them illiterate peasants, serfs, and even slaves, who rarely traveled 10 miles (16 kilometers) from their birthplaces, and barely understood what lands and peoples lay 100 miles (161 kilometers) away. They went to bed at dark and awoke at dawn, because candles were too expensive for people of modest means. They worked in fields and forests with hand tools like hoes and axes; ate

A THRESHING MACHINE IN USE IN 1914. FARM MACHINERY POWERED BY STEAM HELPED TO TRANSFORM AGRICULTURE. IT MADE POSSIBLE THE HUGE "INDUSTRIAL" FARMS OF TODAY, WHICH PRODUCE VAST AMOUNTS OF FOOD, MUCH MORE THAN THE FAMILY FARMS OF THE PAST WERE ABLE TO.

mostly grain in the form of bread, rice, and pudding; had vegetables only in the summer, fruit in the fall, and meat on holidays. Their clothes were simple shapeless dresses and smocks made of cloth woven at home from thread made on hand-driven spinning wheels. They lived constantly frightened of the presence of devils, spirits, and goblins whom they believed to be everywhere around them.

We need only compare that world with our own to see how much human life has been changed by the Industrial Revolution, which brought us airplanes, automobiles, skyscrapers, and all of the electronic entertainment systems that occupy so much of our time. Because of the Industrial Revolution, we not only dress and eat differently from earlier people, we think and even feel differently about the world around us.

When Thomas Newcomen was born, power for industrial purposes was supplied by wind, water, or animals like horses and oxen that could be driven round and round in circles to turn crude machines. Windmills were most often used for pumping water to irrigate fields or drain low-lying areas. The Netherlands became famous for windmills because much of its land was below sea level and was frequently flooded.

But windmills worked only when the wind was blowing, which meant that they could not be used efficiently in a mill needing continuous power. Most factories of Newcomen's time were driven by waterwheels spun by the rush of streams or rivers. But waterwheels had their drawbacks, too. For one, water-driven mills had to be located near rivers, which were usually in the countryside at some distance from transportation and business centers. For another, rivers and streams could flood, dry up, and—in northern climates where the Industrial Revolution began—freeze in winter. For a third, the power of waterwheels was limited. They could turn only as fast as the water flowing over or under them. Waterwheels were nonetheless able to drive a good deal of machinery: by the late 1700s large textile factories were being run by them. However, waterwheels could produce only a fraction of the power needed for a modern industrial plant.

For increased power they needed something else—steam. For two hundred years, the Industrial Revolution was driven by it. Without the steam engine, it would have been impossible.

Steam had aroused the curiosity of thinkers and philosophers going well back in human history. One Greek, Hero of Alexandria, who lived in about 100 C.E., invented a device that spun from the force of steam. One historian says that some of the early Greek and Roman engineers "possessed a remarkable knowledge of the properties of steam." However, they did nothing practical with that knowledge. It has remained one of the great unanswered questions of history why the brilliant theorists of earlier times, not just in Europe but elsewhere in the world, failed to apply their understanding of steam practically.

By the 1600s in Europe, when the boom in science was gathering speed, a few people were trying to see what they could do with steam. An Italian named Giambattista della Porta in 1606 worked out a device

IN THE PAST, WINDMILLS WERE IMPORTANT MACHINES, USED FOR GRINDING GRAIN INTO FLOUR AND MOST OFTEN FOR PUMPING WATER FOR IRRIGATION OR TO DRAIN LOW-LYING AREAS.

SAMUEL MORLAND WAS REPUTED TO HAVE DEVISED A STEAM-DRIVEN MACHINE THAT COULD BE USED TO PUMP WATER, BUT IT IS UNCERTAIN IF HE EVER ACTUALLY PUT IT INTO USE.

that used steam to push water up a pipe. Salomon de Caus in England built a similar device soon after, which he used to work fountains in the gardens of an English prince.

But progress was slow. Sometime around 1680, it is possible that a man named Samuel Morland, who was master of mechanics to the English king Charles II, designed a steam-driven machine that raised and lowered a piston in a cylinder. Such a system could have been used to turn a wheel by means of a rack and pinion. However, it was probably never built.

The principle of the Morland device—using steam pressure to push a piston through a cylinder—is the one we generally think of when we consider engines. But the steam engine developed by Newcomen and improved by Watt used a different principle. For that we must turn to the subject of atmospheric pressure.

Humans have long understood that they are surrounded by an invisible substance called air. They could use it to extinguish a candle or, inversely, increase the heat of a fire. They could feel it on their faces when it moved; they could see it tossing the branches of trees or filling the sails of ships. What it was, exactly, they did not know for sure.

It was, however, a form of matter. When Isaac Newton worked out the laws of gravity, several thinkers realized that air—like Newton's famous apple—had to also be pulled toward the earth. In simple terms, air had weight.

The man who first tried to find out exactly how much air weighed was Otto von Guericke, a German who eventually became mayor of the town of Magdeburg. There was growing interest in the concept and properties of vacuums, and in 1654 Guericke developed an air pump to create vacuums. In one experiment, he had two copper hemispheres made. He fitted them together to make a globe, sealed the joint, and pumped the air out of it. As an audience of noble ladies and gentlemen gaped in astonishment, Guericke showed that eight horses attached to each half of the globe could not pull the two halves apart.

EVANGELISTA TORRICELLI WAS AN IMPORTANT PHYSICIST AND MATHEMATICIAN WHO SUC-
CEEDED THE GREAT GALILEO GALILEI AS PROFESSOR OF MATHEMATICS AT THE UNIVERSITY IN
FLORENCE, ITALY. TORRICELLI DID IMPORTANT WORK ON VACUUMS AND AIR PRESSURE AS
WELL AS ON MICROSCOPES AND TELESCOPES.

At about the same time, a pupil of Galileo's named Evangelista Torricelli also became interested in vacuums. He knew that under normal circumstances a suction pump could raise water to a height only of 32 feet (9.8 meters). He concluded that this was because the air above the water, outside the pump, could displace only its own weight in water.

To give a simple example, suppose you dip an ordinary drinking straw into a can of soda. Nothing happens—that is, the soda will not rise up the straw. This is because the air above is bearing down equally on the soda inside and outside of the straw. Now, if you suck the air out of the straw, there is air pressing down on the soda outside the straw, but none bearing down on the soda inside the straw. The soda outside the straw will be forced by air pressure up into the straw.

Torricelli reasoned that heavier liquids would not be drawn as high up into a glass tube as light ones would. He tried the experiment with mercury, which is heavier than water. Sure enough, the mercury did not rise as far in the glass tube as water did.

These experiments awakened the curiosity of the great French thinker Blaise Pascal. He said that if Torricelli was right, water in a glass vacuum tube would rise higher at sea level than on a mountaintop, simply because there is less air above the mountaintop. In 1648 he asked a friend, who lived near a small mountain, to perform the experiment. Once again the liquid in the glass tube rose higher at the base of the mountain than at its top.

By the time Thomas Newcomen was born, it was well understood that the pressure of air would force substances into vacuums. A vacuum could produce movement, but how did you create a vacuum? Air pumps existed, like the ones Guericke had built, but they worked too slowly to produce a continuous stream of movement. Some people tried creating vacuums by exploding gunpowder in containers, which forced the air out, but nobody could figure out a way to make this system practical.

MANY PEOPLE CONTRIBUTED TO THE EARLY DEVELOPMENT OF THE STEAM ENGINE. ONE WAS DENIS PAPIN, A FRENCHMAN WHO DID SOME OF HIS WORK IN LONDON. HE MADE A MODEL OF A MACHINE THAT USED AIR PRESSURE AND STEAM TO MOVE A PISTON IN A CYLINDER.

Finally, sometime in the 1690s, a Frenchman living in London named Denis Papin worked out a way to create a vacuum using steam. Papin's device used a piston in a cylinder. A small amount of water was placed in the cylinder and heated. The resulting steam drove the piston forward where it was held by a catch. The cylinder was then cooled, so that the steam condensed, leaving a vacuum. When the catch was released, the piston was driven back along the cylinder by the pressure of the air around it. In experiments Papin showed that his piston could lift a fairly large metal weight. He was the first to demonstrate the principle of what came to be called the atmospheric steam engine, because it was driven by the atmosphere, or air.

The first person to attempt a practical atmospheric steam engine was Thomas Savery, an Englishman. In 1699 he demonstrated a machine that powered a water pump. As we have seen, Savery's steam engines were ineffective except for small operations, like pumping a fountain. And by this time Thomas Newcomen was interesting himself in the whole idea.

Newcomen was born in 1663. Some of his ancestors had been well-to-do squires. One branch had owned a large manor house for more than four hundred years. Newcomen's branch, however, had come down in the world. His father was a merchant living in Dartmouth, a seaport town in the southwest of England, not far from Plymouth. The father owned at least one ship, which he used for trading in the Mediterranean and elsewhere. The family was not wealthy, but it was comfortable.

Unfortunately, little is known of Newcomen's youth. He may have been apprenticed to an ironmonger in nearby Exeter, but that is not certain. By 1688 he was back in Dartmouth working as an ironmonger. As such, he would have sold various metal objects like locks, latches, and nails. Some of these items he probably made in his own shop, while others he purchased ready-made for resale. He also bought fairly large quantities of iron, both for resale and for his own use. By the 1690s he was working in partnership with a younger man, John Calley, who would in time help him building steam engines.

At the time, mining was becoming an increasing source of wealth for England. Since the days of the Roman empire, there had been tin mines in Cornwall, in the southwestern corner of the country, not far from Dartmouth. (Tin is essential for making bronze, a metal widely used in ancient times.) Other kinds of mines, like iron-ore mines, were also in the British Isles. More important, there were coal mines. In time, coal would become one of the bases on which the British empire was built,

ONE OF THE EARLIEST USES OF RAILS FOR TRANSPORT WAS IN COAL MINES. HERE, A COAL CART ON RAILS COASTS DOWNHILL AS THE DRIVER SITS ON THE BRAKE HANDLE TO SLOW THE CART DOWN. THE HORSE WALKS ALONG BEHIND.

used not only in England for factories and dwellings, but exported and sold abroad.

Initially, mines had been close to the surface. Top layers of dirt would be removed, uncovering the minerals, which could then be dug out. However, many minerals are found deep underground randomly deposited in veins. By Newcomen's time, mine shafts had been pushed deep into the earth in vast systems of twisting tunnels.

Unfortunately, there are not only coal, iron, and tin underground, but water. Over time, many of these mines flooded. Frequently, the flooding was so bad that portions, or even all, of the mine was "drowned" as the saying was. The mine had to be closed, with much loss of money. Mine owners worked out various pumping systems, mainly using horses for power, but these systems were not always effective. Horse-driven pumps were not powerful enough to clear deep mines; moreover, horses were expensive to feed and care for. As a result, many drowned mines stayed filled with water. Everybody knew that if they could be emptied, a great amount of valuable coal and other minerals could be recovered.

It is almost certain that Newcomen was doing business with the tin miners of Cornwall, presumably selling them metal parts and fittings for their hoists, horse-driven pumps, and other machinery. He was well acquainted with the problem of flooding in mines. And, clearly, he knew about the well-promoted attempts of Thomas Savery and others to use steam to pump water. Sometime in the 1690s, he decided to see if he could build a steam pump of his own.

We know next to nothing about the early stages of Newcomen's experiments. He did not keep careful records of them as scientists are trained to do. He simply tried this or that to see what would work and then went on to the next problem. Nor did he in old age sit down to write a memoir. We have almost nothing from Newcomen himself about how he developed his steam engine.

We can say for certain that by 1712 Newcomen had produced at least one working steam engine. He may have produced an earlier one, perhaps even two, but they could not have been built much before 1712. We also are fairly sure that he had been working on steam engines for at least ten years before 1712, probably with the assistance of John Calley.

We know how these early Newcomen engines worked. There may not have been much attention paid to Newcomen, but there was substantial interest in the innovations of the time. We are so used to living in a world full of machines operating on their "own steam," as we still say (many of them, like refrigerators, that run continuously for twenty years at a stretch), that we forget how novel the idea was three hundred years ago. Since the invention of clocks and watches, no human being had invented any automatic, self-powered machine that wasn't driven by wind or water. The steam engine was not merely a new source of power; it was the first true machine of any kind, if we can discount the limited system of clockwork that already existed.

As a result, many descriptions and illustrations of various of Newcomen's engines were published and sold to the public. These illustrations sometimes contained inaccuracies, but on the whole they were very good and give us an excellent idea of how Newcomen's steam engines worked.

They were not built in a factory, but were constructed one piece at a time on the spot, at the opening of the mine shaft, mainly from parts previously manufactured elsewhere. Each one was tailor-made for the particular mine. Furthermore, Newcomen, and others, were constantly tinkering with the design of the engines to make improvements. As a result, the steam engines varied in both size and detail.

However, they generally operated according to the same plan. To start with, there was a large boiler—usually a few feet in diameter, often made of copper—with a dome-shaped lead top. Beneath the boiler was the furnace, which burned coal, cheap and easy to get at the coal mines but more expensive at the tin mines.

Above the boiler rose a tall cylinder made of brass. At first these cylinders were relatively small in diameter, under 3 feet (0.9 meter),

AN EARLY SKETCH OF A NEWCOMEN STEAM ENGINE, TAKEN FROM A MAGAZINE OF THE DAY.
THE LEFT END OF THE ROCKER ARM IS ATTACHED BY A CHAIN OR A ROD TO THE PISTON
LODGED INSIDE THE CYLINDER. WHEN THE STEAM IN THE CYLINDER WAS SUDDENLY COOLED,
IT CONDENSED, OR RETURNED TO LIQUID FORM. THE VACUUM THAT WAS THEN CREATED
PULLED THE PISTON DOWN AND THE LEFT END OF THE ROCKER ARM WITH IT. WHEN THE
VACUUM WAS BROKEN, THE WEIGHT OF THE PUMPING MACHINE, ATTACHED TO THE
RIGHT END OF THE ROCKER ARM, PULLED THE ARM BACK DOWN INTO THE POSITION SHOWN
IN THE SKETCH.

A MODEL OF A NEWCOMEN STEAM ENGINE. THE CONE-SHAPED OBJECT IS THE BOILER IN WHICH WATER WAS HEATED TO CREATE STEAM. ON TOP OF THE BOILER IS THE CYLINDER IN WHICH THE PISTON MOVED UP AND DOWN.

but over time they became gigantic, sometimes 6 or 7 feet (1.8 or 2.1 meters) in diameter and 10 feet (3 meters) long. The bigger the system, the more powerful it became and the more water it could pump.

Inside the cylinder was a piston, generally shaped like a huge disk, perhaps 1 foot (0.3 meter) or more thick. One of the biggest problems in building steam engines was to make the piston fit tightly in the cylinder so that steam pressure did not escape around the piston. The casting and grinding of metal was still an imprecise craft. In one documented case, the maker of one of Newcomen's cylinders ground it by having a huge lead plug cast to the diameter of the cylinder bore. Grit was spread over the interior surface of the cylinder. Then several men, using ropes, pulled the lead plug back and forth inside the cylinder, thus polishing it with the grit. Needless to say, such a method could produce a cylinder that was only approximately round. The way the cylinder fitted inside the piston was usually far from perfect. To help contain the steam, Newcomen placed a piece of wet leather on top of the piston to help fill gaps between the piston and the cylinder wall. He also discovered that a thin layer of water on top of the piston helped to contain the steam.

The piston was attached by a sturdy chain to an overhead rocker arm, a huge wooden beam perhaps 30 feet (9.2 meters) long and 2 or 3 feet (0.6 or 0.9 meter) thick. This beam was set perhaps 20 feet (6.1 meters) above the ground on a strong brick wall, usually one of the walls of the boiler house, where it seesawed up and down with the movement of the engine. Attached to the other end of the beam, or rocker arm, was a rod that descended the mine shaft to the pump. When the engine was in operation, steam from the boiler was sent into the cylinder. Then a jet of cold water was shot in. The steam immediately condensed, creating a vacuum. The piston was instantly driven down by the pressure of the air above it—sucked down exactly as soda is sucked up through a straw. The beam then rocked downward, pulling the pump rod at the other end upward. Steam was reintroduced into the cylinder, breaking the vacuum, and the weight of the pump rod rocked the beam back the other way, lifting the piston.

We must realize that the piston was not driven upward by steam pressure; it rose because the great weight of the pumping mechanism on the other end of the rocker arm pulled it. The work was done first by the vacuum and then by the weight of the pumping equipment—that is, first by the pull of gravity on the air and then by the pull of gravity on the pump rods.

This sounds as if it must have been a very slow process, but in fact, by the time Newcomen had improved his engine, it could make up to twelve or fifteen strokes a minute, or one stroke every four or five seconds. So the piston was traveling at about the rate of 2 feet (0.6 meter) per second, depending on the size of the machine, or at about the speed of somebody marching.

Originally, in the earliest steam engines, like the ones built by Thomas Savery, a boy was employed to open a valve to let steam into the cylinder at the right moment and then to open another one to let the jet of cooling water in a few seconds later. This was tedious work that required careful timing. One of Newcomen's great improvements was to develop a system of levers by which these valves were opened

MUCH OF THE WORK DONE IN COAL MINES WAS ORIGINALLY PERFORMED BY HAND. HERE, WOMEN CARRY BASKETS OF COAL TO THE SURFACE. THE WOMAN AT THE TOP HAS LOST PART OF HER LOAD, WHICH MAY COME CRASHING ONTO THE WOMAN BELOW. SERIOUS INJURY WAS COMMONPLACE IN THE MINES OF THE TIME. THE INTRODUCTION OF THE STEAM ENGINE AND OTHER MACHINERY EASED THE WORK, ALTHOUGH THE LIFE OF A MINER WAS STILL HARD.

and closed at the proper times by the movement of the machine itself. With automatic valves, the machine was truly self-driven: as long as the boiler was supplied with water, and the boiler furnace was fed coal, it would go on running without human intervention until it wore out.

The steam engine was much more complex than the description given here, but it conveys the basic principles. Newcomen's machines may have worked slowly, but for their day they had enormous power. They could draw thousands of gallons of water an hour from mines of great depth. Despite the expense in building them, they were much cheaper to operate than horse-drawn pumps. They also quickly paid for themselves. Effective and economical, they were rapidly put into operation. Newcomen himself set up perhaps one hundred of them, and at least 1,500 more were built by others in the eighteenth century, not just in Great Britain, but throughout Europe and in America. The Newcomen engine vastly increased the amount of coal available to Europeans and so was critical in giving the Industrial Revolution its start.

THIS ROMANTIC IMAGE SHOWS JAMES WATT AS A BOY OBSERVING STEAM COMING FROM A TEAPOT, WHILE A WOMAN, PRESUMABLY HIS MOTHER, HOLDS A WATCH. IT IS UNLIKELY THAT WATT'S INTEREST IN STEAM ENGINES BEGAN IN THIS FASHION, THOUGH HE WAS AN OBSERVANT BOY, CURIOUS ABOUT THE NATURAL PHENOMENA OCCURRING AROUND HIM.

Enter James Watt

It is unquestionable that Newcomen, not James Watt, built the first practical steam engine. However, it is also true that Watt made such significant improvements in Newcomen's machine that he opened the way for a much wider use of steam and thus gave the new industrial world a second push forward.

James Watt was born in 1736 in Greenock, on the Firth of Clyde, in what would become an important industrial area of Scotland. He was, according to one historian, a "delicate, studious lad." Many of his relatives were surveyors, and Watt grew up with a mechanical bent. He eventually went to London to learn how to make mathematical instruments. In those days, people did not specialize as much as we do today, and he soon branched out into general engineering.

Almost by chance, in 1763 Watt was asked to repair a Newcomen-type atmospheric steam engine in use at Glasgow University, not far from his home. While Newcomen had little formal training in mathematics, Watt had a strong background in the subject. Applying appropriate thermodynamic formulas, Watt quickly saw that the atmospheric steam engine was exceedingly inefficient in the way it used heat. In the Newcomen system, steam in the cylinder was suddenly condensed by a jet of cold water. Watt realized that the cylinder was being continually heated and cooled again and again several times a minute. Too much fuel was lost or wasted in this cycle of ever-fluctuating temperatures.

A PORTRAIT OF MATTHEW BOULTON, WHO WAS TYPICAL OF THE BUSINESSMEN WHO GREW RICH FROM THE NEW INDUSTRIAL SYSTEM HE AND OTHERS HELPED TO BRING ABOUT.

He mused on the problem, and one day he saw the answer. If the steam could be drawn out of the cylinder and condensed elsewhere, the cylinder itself could be kept hot until the next batch of steam was introduced, with a vast saving in fuel. So Watt added a condenser to this system—which is basically a container attached to one side of the cylinder. Allowing the cylinder to remain hot meant 75 percent less coal was needed, making steam engines much cheaper to run.

Watt also worked out a system in which steam was introduced to the upper side of the piston, which gave it added power. These, and other improvements, took Watt some ten years to develop. By 1770 word was out that James Watt was creating a substantially better steam engine than the Newcomen system. Matthew Boulton, the industrial leader of the English Midlands, still a great manufacturing center, heard about the new machine. He decided to back Watt, at least in part because he wanted the more efficient engine for his own factories. They formed a company called Boulton and Watt, which would make them rich and famous. On May 8, 1776, they began to operate the first of the new Watt steam engines at the Bloomfield Colliery. The success of the machine was immediate. By 1800 Boulton and Watt had made almost five hundred of their improved steam engines.

The Watt machine, however important, was still basically an improvement on the original Newcomen atmospheric steam engine. It worked by rocking a beam back and forth. This up-and-down motion was suitable for pumping water, and for a few other purposes, but for most other industrial purposes a machine that spun a wheel was essential. Wagon wheels, ship paddle wheels, windlasses, and hoists all depended on the rotation of a spinning wheel. Boulton began putting pressure on Watt to produce a rotative steam engine.

As it happened, much of the technology was available. As early as 1740 an Englishman named John Wise had suggested the use of a flywheel—a large, relatively heavy wheel attached to an engine, which would provide momentum to keep the machine moving at a steady pace. In 1779 Matthew Wasborough added one to a steam engine. About the same time James Pickard added a crank. The idea of the crank was not new; the pedal of a bicycle wheel is a crank, with the rider's legs acting as connecting rods. Soon Watt had developed his own rotative steam engine, which the rocking beam raised and lowered a rod, just as the leg of a bicycle rider pumps up and down. And just as the bicycle pedal spins the wheel, so the crank spun a wheel or axle.

The rotative steam engine was quickly set to work driving all sorts of equipment—winches for hoisting coal out of mines, belt-run pulleys for rolling iron, grinding sugarcane, and for driving spinning, weaving and other machines in textile factories. In 1812 Richard Trevithick devised a steam machine for threshing wheat. Soon other agricultural machines

THIS PORTRAIT OF JAMES WATT, PROBABLY PAINTED IN 1792, SHOWS THE INVENTOR IN A THOUGHTFUL POSE. BESIDE HIM IS A SKETCH OF A ROTATIVE STEAM ENGINE, THE DEVICE THAT PROVED SO IMPORTANT TO THE INDUSTRIAL REVOLUTION.

followed; steam machines of various kinds were being used on large farms well into the twentieth century. In the 1820s a man named Jacob Perkins demonstrated a steam-driven machine gun to the Duke of Wellington: balls dropped out of a funnel or hopper and were fired by steam at the rate of one thousand per minute. The balls were able to penetrate eleven wood planks that were each 1 inch (2.5 centimeters) thick and were set 1 inch apart. Probably because the weapon was too cumbersome, it was never used. Later, before the development of the gasoline-powered internal-combustion engine, attempts were made to use steam engines to propel airplanes. The engines proved too heavy.

The main use of the steam engine was to drive machinery, especially manufacturing machines in the new industries that were rapidly being born in the 1800s. The movement away from waterwheels to steam had an immense impact on the way humans lived. Factories could now be built in cities instead of along country rivers. They were closer to shipping docks and road junctions, making the delivery of raw materials and the shipping of finished goods vastly more efficient. It meant, moreover, that for better or worse, millions of workers had to move to cities to find jobs. Cities rapidly expanded as a new urban way of living was created. This caused many problems. For one, even by the mid-1700s, many were protesting the amount of pollution, in the form of coal smoke, that the new steam machines were spewing. One of the advantages of the Watt improvements, it was thought, was that with greater fuel efficiency, there would be less smoke pollution. Nobody realized that this very efficiency would encourage an upsurge in steam-engine use and ever-increasing air pollution.

In addition, most factory workers, many of them children as young as twelve, were paid very low wages, were forced to work long hours, and lived with their families in cramped apartments in neighborhoods where disease and crime were rampant.

But the new steam-run industry produced greater material wealth, as well. To take just one example, before machines, a hand weaver

A DRAWING OF CHILDREN WORKING IN A TEXTILE FACTORY IN ABOUT 1820. THE PICTURE DOES NOT EXAGGER-ATE THE CIRCUMSTANCES: CHILDREN WERE PARTICULARLY SOUGHT FOR WORK IN TEXTILE PLANTS AS THEIR SMALL FINGERS WERE ADEPT AT TYING THREAD. CHILDREN CONTINUED TO BE EMPLOYED IN SUCH FACTORIES INTO THE TWENTIETH CENTURY, BOTH IN EUROPE AND THE UNITED STATES.

could turn out two pieces of shirt fabric 24 yards (22 meters) long each week. By 1833 a teenaged steam loom weaver with a twelve-year-old assistant could produce ten times as much. (As this suggests, the use of child labor in the nineteenth century was one of the great abuses of the industrial system.)

The most visible part of the steam revolution came in transportation, always a matter of great concern to humans. There are often found in the remains of Stone Age settlements minerals and fossilized foodstuffs that could not have been obtained locally, but must have been brought from great distances. The great stones making up the famous Stonehenge in England, built between 3100 and 1600 B.C.E., were wrestled from mountains more than 200 miles (322 kilometers) away. Two thousand years ago, Romans were shipping goods to their capital from a huge empire that stretched from Egypt to England. And by the twelfth century C.E., Europeans were sending trading ships farther and farther, first around the Mediterranean and then along the Atlantic coast.

It is no accident that the Industrial Revolution began in England, whose leaders recognized that, as a small island nation, it could not build vast wealth simply on what could be produced at home. For them, the plan was to bring in raw materials from elsewhere and then to manufacture them into finished goods that could be sold to the rest of the world. With financial awards, the British government actively encouraged inventions and innovations in technology. It also set up patent rules that enabled inventors to have exclusive rights to sell their creations for a number of years, but let others capitalize on them after a reasonable amount of time had passed.

The English were also busy building a great colonial empire, which in Newcomen's day included the American colonies, and which would eventually stretch around the globe. Cotton pouring in from India, Egypt, and America was turned into cloth. Timber from Canada and the West Indies became elegant furniture. Sugar and tobacco from the Caribbean and the American South were processed exclusively in Great Britain, as American planters were not allowed to sell their tobacco to other nations, but had to ship it to London. Silver from Africa was turned into tea sets and tableware. Other nations, especially France, were trying to do the same, but none was as successful as the English.

This huge mercantile system was based on ships, canal barges, and carts and wagons drawn by animals, mainly horses. But animals were

IN THIS TEXTILE FACTORY, A BOY IS EMPLOYED TO CREEP UNDER THE THREADS TO SWEEP THE PLACES AN ADULT COULD NOT REACH.

expensive to feed and often grew lame and ill. Sailing ships could become becalmed in dead air for days, even weeks, at a time. The Atlantic crossing from the cotton plantations of Virginia to the spinning mills of Birmingham might take as long as three months. In particular, coal, essential to industry, had to be carried in vast quantities from mines to mills.

It soon occurred to people that it might be possible to run a ship by steam. The new, efficient Watt steam engine could be made a lot smaller than the old Newcomen pumper, which was usually far too large to be portable. The Watt machine required much less coal and water; boilers could be smaller.

The first person to actually build a working steamboat was an American, John Fitch. Fitch's boat was rowed by pairs of oars driven by steam. He ran it successfully on the Delaware River near Philadelphia in 1787. In the same year, James Rumsey demonstrated a steamboat on the Potomac River. Rumsey's boat was propelled by a jet of water forced out of the stern by steam. Fitch followed up with several small steamboats, one of which could travel at 8 miles (12.9 kilometers) per hour, a promising speed. He actually operated it as a commercial venture out of Philadelphia. However, his backers would not provide him with enough financing, his company soon failed, and, discouraged, he committed suicide.

But the potential for steamboats was clear, and other people took up the challenge. One of these was Robert Fulton, another American, who got backing in France and in 1803 launched a steamboat there. In the same year in Scotland, a stern paddle wheeler named the *Charlotte Dundas*, after the backer's daughter, was launched. Its engine did not have a rocking beam; the piston was hitched directly to the paddle wheel by means of a crank. Used to haul two barges along the Forth and Clyde Canal, on its maiden voyage it traveled almost 20 miles (32.2 kilometers) in six hours. This was about as fast as a horse could walk with a heavy load, but the *Charlotte Dundas* was hauling a far heavier load than a horse could drag over rough roads.

The real turning point came in 1807 when Fulton, now back in the United States, launched the very successful steamboat known today as the *Clermont*, but originally registered as the *North River Steamboat of Clermont*. It was 150 feet (45.8 meters) long and 13 feet (4 meters) wide. It used a Boulton and Watt engine. A large L-shaped beam, pivoting at the angle, acted as the crank. The first

ROBERT FULTON WITH THE *CLERMONT* PICTURED BEHIND HIM.

THE *COMET*, A PADDLE-WHEEL STEAMBOAT BUILT IN GLASGOW, SCOTLAND. IT WAS USED TO HAUL FREIGHT AND PASSENGERS IN THE GLASGOW AREA.

commercial voyage of the *Clermont* came on September 4, 1807. On its first trip, the *Clermont* traveled from New York City up the Hudson River to Albany, a distance of 150 miles (241.5 kilometers), at an average speed of about 5 miles (8 kilometers) per hour.

In the same year a British ship, the *Comet,* built by Henry Bell, was launched. Nobody knew it yet, but the sailing vessel, which had been used by humans for at least eight thousand years, was in its twilight years. Within the span of a lifetime, it would be used only for fun.

Although the steamboat soon started being used in many places, it was of particular importance to Americans. In Europe, China, and elsewhere, road systems had been under construction for at least two thousand years and in some places much longer. The American Indians, however, had neither horses nor the wheel until the arrival of Europeans in the 1500s, and they did not really begin to adopt carts and wagons until the 1800s. Road building in North America only began in earnest in the 1600s, and much of the continent remained unmarked by roads for another two hundred years.

As a consequence, water routes were the highways of their day. The continent was crossed by great rivers—the Mississippi, the Missouri, the Ohio, the Hudson, the Delaware, and many more. There were also large lakes and the long coastline stretching from the North Atlantic to the Gulf of Mexico. It was far quicker to move goods and people over water than through forests over uneven roads on which a horse and a cart would be lucky to make 1 mile (1.6 kilometers) an hour.

Americans needed more transportation routes. Their primary products were not manufactured goods coming out of factories, but raw materials—cotton, tobacco, wheat, salted cod, smoked pork, timber, and animal hides. Manufactured goods like clocks, glasses, and silverware were relatively expensive per pound, so that a small shipment of them could bring a considerable profit. Wheat, cotton, and similar crops, on the other hand, were cheap and had to be shipped in large quantities to bring in much money.

Water transport was cheap but slow, and many rivers flooded in the spring, grew shallow in the fall, and in the North froze in the winter. Furthermore, while it was easy enough to maneuver a boat downstream at a fair speed, it was another thing to sail or row one upstream against the current. Making matters worse, rivers like the Hudson were tidal, sometimes for a distance of 100 miles (161 kilometers) or more upriver: tides shifting twice a day increased the problem of currents.

A steamboat, however, could move rapidly upstream. So in the United States steamboats took over. In 1817, only ten years after the first voyage of the *Clermont*, there were seventeen steamboats on the Mississippi; three years later there were sixty-nine. During that period, a new steamboat was launched on the Mississippi alone every three weeks,

THE ROMANCE OF THE STEAMBOAT WAS CAPTURED BY WRITER MARK TWAIN IN HIS CLASSIC *LIFE ON THE MISSISSIPPI*. MOST STEAMBOATS WERE ORNATE AND CARRIED PASSENGERS IN STYLE AND COMFORT. HERE, TWO STEAMBOATS RACE ON THE MISSISSIPPI RIVER, ALWAYS A RISKY ACTIVITY.

and many more were launched elsewhere. American steamboats were cheap to run, for they usually burned wood, rather than coal. There was an endless supply of wood in the forests along many rivers so, unlike coal, wood reserves did not have to be carried far to get to the ships. Along the major rivers, where steamboats constantly passed, farmers would cut and stack huge piles of wood along the banks; a steamer could simply pull alongshore and load up.

Within two decades, the rivers of the United States were aswarm with steamboats. The Mississippi riverboats were especially a subject of much romance. By the 1840s they had become elegant floating palaces with gilt decorations, shining brass rails and fixtures, and cut-glass chandeliers in the dining rooms. The Mississippi River pilot was a figure of great glamour who earned a substantial salary for doing work that boys all over America envied.

Of course it was dangerous. Riverboats often ran aground on shifting sands hidden just below the water's surface or tore their bottoms on huge uprooted trees invisible in the dark. Sometimes foolhardy captains challenged each other to races. To increase pressure, the safety valve on the boiler would be tied down, and often enough the boiler exploded, scalding many of the crew and passengers to death. But the risks only made the life of the pilot that much more glamorous. One of the classic works of American literature is Mark Twain's story of the steamboats, *Life on the Mississippi*.

The first Atlantic crossing using steam came in 1819 when the *Savannah* ran from the United States to England. It mainly traveled by sail, but used steam when the winds fell. In 1838 the venturesome engineer and designer Isambard Kingdom Brunel launched two paddle-wheel steamers that raced across the Atlantic. One of them proved too small for regular service, but the *Great Western* continued to run between Bristol, England, and New York City until 1846. In 1843 Brunel launched another important vessel, the *Great Britain*. This ship was the first transatlantic liner to employ the screw propeller, which had been invented by a Swedish engineer, John Ericsson, in 1836. The

ISAMBARD KINGDOM BRUNEL'S SHIP *GREAT BRITAIN* WAS THE FIRST TO CROSS THE ATLANTIC USING THE SCREW PROPELLER RATHER THAN PADDLE WHEELS. SAILS COULD BE USED TO SAVE COAL WHEN THE WINDS WERE FAVORABLE.

screw was a far more efficient device than the paddle wheel for pushing a ship through water, and it quickly took over.

The new seagoing steamships dramatically shortened the Atlantic journey. Where sailing ships might take three months to cross, depending on wind and weather, the propeller-driven steamships could make the trip in two weeks. In 1863 the last paddle wheeler to be launched, the *Scotia,* set an Atlantic record of eight days and three hours. Today large ocean liners can make the trip in fewer than four days.

Furthermore, steam allowed bigger ships to be built, which could carry hundreds, and eventually thousands, of passengers. In 1620 the *Mayflower* carried just more than one hundred people to Massachusetts; Brunel's *Great Britain* could carry 360; and by the 1880s ships with hundreds of passengers jammed into steerage were crossing the Atlantic in ten days or less.

Prices for the Atlantic crossing fell. Cheap steamship tickets allowed millions of Europeans to make the Atlantic crossing to immigrate to America—mostly to the United States, but many to Canada and South America. So steam was an important factor in creating the great wave of immigration that came to the United States in the nineteenth and early twentieth centuries. Not only did it permit cheap travel, but it was crucial to building the industrial machines that provided jobs for the new arrivals. The steam engine had played a pivotal role in making and shaping the modern world.

THIS PICTURE SHOWS THE CUGNOT STEAM TRACTOR HITTING A WALL DURING ITS FIRST TRIAL RUN. THE ACCIDENT DISCOURAGED THE FRENCH GOVERNMENT FROM INVESTING FURTHER IN THE INVENTOR'S MACHINE. THE BOILER IN FRONT FED STEAM TO THE CYLINDER JUST BEHIND IT, WHICH IN TURN MOVED A BICYCLELIKE CRANK TO TURN THE WHEEL. THIS MACHINE CAN BE SEEN TODAY IN A MUSEUM IN PARIS.

The Railroads

Just as it had occurred to some people in the eighteenth century that it might be possible to move ships by steam, still others came to realize that it could also be used to propel wagons and carriages. However, although a ship had room for a fairly large steam engine and the fuel it needed, a wagon or carriage did not. Fulton's *Clermont* was 150 feet (45.8 meters) long and 9 feet (2.7 meters) deep; no cart that large could be built.

Yet, before the introduction of the Watt steam engine, at least one man succeeded in building what can best be called a steam tractor. He was Nicolas-Joseph Cugnot. One of the biggest problems facing military commanders, in the various wars that plagued Europe, was moving field artillery rapidly from place to place, either to bring cannons into position to fire on swiftly moving enemy troops or to escape them when a battle was going badly.

Cugnot decided to build a steam tractor for hauling cannons. In 1769 he constructed a prototype and got backing from the French ministry of war. He then made a large vehicle with one wheel in front and two in the rear. It had a large boiler mounted on the front and was altogether a strange-looking creature. In 1770 he tested it and found it worked. Unfortunately, during the trial run it accidentally hit a wall and was damaged. The war minister withdrew his support, which ended

RICHARD TREVITHICK BUILT THE FIRST STEAM ENGINE THAT COULD RUN ON RAILS, AS WELL AS ANOTHER MODEL THAT RAN ALONG ROADS. BUT HE NEVER FOLLOWED THROUGH ON HIS INVENTIONS, AND ONLY RECENTLY HAS HE BEEN GIVEN THE CREDIT HE DESERVES FOR HIS GROUNDBREAKING INNOVATIONS.

Cugnot's experiment. He died poor and forgotten in 1804. However, his steam tractor was preserved and can be seen today in the Musée d'Arts et Métier in Paris.

Cugnot's legacy was to show that traveling on land by steam was possible. The first to try again was Richard Trevithick, the same Englishman who invented the threshing machine. Just as students of history have always believed that Watt invented the steam engine, so we believe that George Stephenson invented the railway locomotive. In fact, the locomotive was invented by Trevithick.

We do not know much about Trevithick. He was born in 1771, at the same time that Watt was working on his improved steam engine. He had some training in engineering and as a young man had a responsible position in the Cornish mines, where so many of Newcomen's steam pumps were then operating. So Trevithick knew a great deal about the inner workings of steam engines.

Probably in about 1798 he began developing a completely new type of steam engine. Newcomen and Watt's earlier systems worked on atmospheric pressure: a vacuum was created in a cylinder into which a piston was pushed by the pressure of the air above it.

Trevithick's idea was to propel the piston by the power of the steam itself. In the atmospheric engine, the weight of the air was doing the work. The steam pressure had to be only powerful enough to force air out of the cylinder. That is, it had to be just slightly greater than air pressure. In the Trevithick system, steam itself provided the power. The steam pressure would have to be much higher to drive the piston and the machinery it was attached to. Ultimately, it was a simpler system, because the steam did not have to be condensed, but could simply escape.

This new high-pressure system needed a boiler with much thicker walls, which would not explode under high pressure. More importantly, it required a lot more heat than the older system. So the high-pressure system was more expensive to run. But, being simpler in design, it was cheaper to manufacture and could be made much smaller than atmospheric engines.

A CARTOON DRAWN IN 1831, ENTITLED "THE PLEASURE OF THE RAIL-ROAD," SHOWS PASSENGERS BLOWN TO BITS BY AN EXPLODING BOILER. IN TRUTH, TRAINS OF THE DAY WERE A LOT SAFER THAN THIS CARTOON SUGGESTS. THE MAIN DANGER WAS FROM COLLISIONS WITH OTHER TRAINS, NOT EXPLODING BOILERS.

As it happens, an American named Oliver Evans had come up with the same idea. In 1804 he produced a high-pressure machine. "I succeeded perfectly with my little engine. I could break and grind 200 bushels of plaster of Paris, or 12 tons, in twenty-four hours." In that year there were only six steam engines in the United States. One authority says that the Americans were fifty years behind the English in mechanical skills. This may, perhaps, be an exaggeration: Americans were already developing the mass-production system of interchangeable parts. But there is no doubt that the Americans were well behind the English industrially. Evans seemed, to people who knew him, a dreamer. The value of what he had done went unrecognized. He was "derided and criticized" and could get nowhere with his ideas.

Back in England, Trevithick was already thinking about using steam to move a carriage. We do not know anything about his first attempts, but on Christmas Eve of 1801 he tried to run a steam-driven carriage up a slight incline in his hometown of Camborne. The attempt failed. He tried again two days later. The carriage moved, but the roughness of the road caused problems. Trevithick and the friends who had witnessed the trial put the carriage in a shed and went off to have dinner. The heat from the boiler caused the shed to catch fire, and everything was destroyed in flames.

But Trevithick, who appears to have been an erratic genius, did not give up. In 1803 he built another steam carriage, which he drove around London on a 4-mile (6.4-kilometer) route several times.

A major problem for both Trevithick and Cugnot, in producing what were actually forerunners to the automobile, was the bumpiness of the roads of that time. Nonetheless, people kept trying to build steam carriages. In 1825 Goldsworthy Gurney tried to avoid the poorly surfaced roads altogether by designing a steam car that walked on legs. Two years later, he built one that traveled on wheels at 15 miles (24.2 kilometers) per hour. In 1833 Walter Hancock put into service two steam buses that could reach 12 miles (19.3 kilometers) per hour and over several years carried some four thousand passengers. But by this time, steam buses and carriages were being made obsolete by another innovation: rails.

The idea of moving cars and wagons on rails was not new. As far back as Roman times, 1,500 years earlier, people realized that a road built mainly for wheeled traffic did not have to be 20 feet (6.1 meters) wide, but could consist of two narrow parallel strips. Wooden, and then metal, rails were created. There is evidence of simple railways existing in the sixteenth century, and undoubtedly there had been earlier ones. A horse that might struggle to pull one cart over uneven roads could easily pull two or three along a system of rails.

As coal mines were dug with ever-lengthening tunnels, there was an increased need for efficient methods of carting coal over thousands of feet of irregular surfaces. Coal also had to be moved aboveground from the mine head to the storehouses or barges that transported it elsewhere. Iron rails were in use for many purposes in collieries by Trevithick's time.

The biggest technical problem with rails was finding ways of keeping the cart wheels on the tracks. Initially, the rails were flanged, or ridged, either on the outer or inner edges. In time, however, the flange was put on the wheel instead of the rail—the system railroad trains use today. Coal carts running on rails were drawn by horses or, in some cases, by people.

In 1803 Trevithick was in south Wales, building engines for ironworks. A mill owner named Samuel Homfray, from a place called Pen-y-darren, bet Anthony Hill, owner of the Plymouth Ironworks, five hundred guineas—a considerable amount of money at the time—that Trevithick could build a locomotive that could run along the railway connecting their ironworks to the Glamorganshire Canal, a shipping point for their goods. Homfray most likely arranged this bet to tempt Trevithick into building a steam locomotive. Whatever the case, within a few weeks Trevithick had accomplished the task. On February 21, 1804, the first railway train ran 9.75 miles (15.7 kilometers) along the Pen-y-darren railway.

THIS DRAWING SHOWS TWO OF THE EARLIEST LOCOMOTIVES, THE PEN-Y-DARREN AND A LATER ONE BUILT BY FRANCIS TREVITHICK IN 1847. THE PEN-Y-DARREN IS ON THE BRIDGE.

Trevithick went on to build a passenger train in London which ran in a circle and carried passengers around and around for a shilling each. A shilling was a day's wages for most workers, and the scheme soon failed for lack of customers. But Trevithick had showed without question that steam could be used to power carriages over land. Had he continued to push forward with his locomotive, he would have undoubtedly earned enduring fame. Today, almost exactly two hundred years after the Pen-y-darren made its first run to meet the conditions of a bet, Trevithick is beginning to get the recognition he deserves.

GEORGE STEPHENSON IS OFTEN CREDITED WITH BEING THE INVENTOR OF THE RAILROAD LOCOMOTIVE. HE WAS NOT, BUT HE WAS RESPONSIBLE FOR BUILDING THE FIRST PRACTICAL RAILWAY SYSTEMS.

It was left to George Stephenson, then, to turn the steam locomotive into a railway system. Stephenson was from the north of England. Like Newcomen, he was more a practical man than a theorist. But unlike Newcomen, he had been trained as an engineer. Along with many people, he was drawn to the exciting new steam engine and was looking for ways to improve on what others had done. Surprisingly, nobody had really followed up on Trevithick's work, although a few steam locomotives were being used in collieries. High-pressure rotative steam engines were now being widely used in industry, and were running steamboats on American rivers. But the steam-powered train barely existed.

Then, in 1821, a group of English businessmen decided to build a horse-drawn railway system from Darlington, an industrial center, to Stockton-on-Tees, a seaport, about 26 miles (41.9 kilometers) away. They asked Stephenson to take charge of it.

Stephenson built the railway as instructed, including carriages to be pulled by horses. But he also built a locomotive, which he called *Locomotion.* The Stockton and Darlington Railway opened in September 1825. It was the first true public railroad: up until then, rail lines had been private, built for the use of mill and mine owners. On opening day *Locomotion,* attached to thirty-three cars, attracted a large crowd. As it was about to set off on the first public railway trip in history, the safety valve lifted, sending out a blast of steam. The crowd broke up and fled in all directions, sure a great explosion was about to take place. There was, however, no eruption, and the *Locomotion* proceeded on a successful journey.

The Stockton and Darlington line carried both passengers and freight, mainly coal. First-class passengers rode in brightly colored cars that resembled ordinary horse-drawn carriages; third-class passengers stood up in what were simply empty cars. A fully loaded train hauling 90 tons (82 metric tons) of freight could get up to speeds of 6 to 8 miles (9.7 to 12.9 kilometers) per hour, but passenger cars made much better time. Horse-drawn passenger cars continued in service until 1833 but were then eliminated. The future belonged to the steam engine.

TWO ENGINES APPROACH ONE ANOTHER ON A SINGLE TRACK, AS THE SIGNAL AT FAR LEFT WARNS THEM OF DANGER. MANY TYPES OF SIGNALING SYSTEMS WERE TRIED BEFORE THE MODERN VERSION WAS DEVELOPED.

From the railroad's earliest days, there was always a good deal of dispute about how tracks ought to be made. Initially, there were no cross ties holding the rails together: ties would have made difficult going for horses, as anyone who has walked along a railroad track knows. Instead the rails were fastened to blocks of wood or stone dug into the ground. However, these supporting blocks tended to shift in the ground, both from the weight of the trains and the effects of weather. Cross ties, or sleepers as they are sometimes called, largely solved this problem, for they each tied the rails together at the correct distance. This is the system used for the huge modern trains of today.

Soon another problem arose. Even these early trains, small by comparison to modern ones, were hard to stop once they got rolling, especially if they were pulling 100 tons (91 metric tons) of coal. Brake systems were also primitive. A driver might not be able to see around a curve that a train ahead of him had broken down and was standing on the track. Thus, signals were set up. In some cases these signals were human—a uniformed man standing beside the track holding his arms in certain ways to warn the driver to slow or stop. However, semaphore signals with wooden or metal arms on tall poles soon became standard. They were not automatic, as they are today, but had to be raised and lowered by ropes and chains by a signalman below.

The Stockton and Darlington Railway was a success. Nonetheless, there was continual trouble with the locomotives. Eventually the locomotive engineer for the line, Timothy Hackworth, devised a new locomotive that had six wheels coupled, or joined by rods so that they all moved in unison, which reduced wheel slippage. Hackworth made other improvements. His resulting engine was the now famous Royal George, named for George IV, the king of England at the time.

The popularity of the Stockton and Darlington Railway encouraged other people to build railway lines when they saw how much money could be made in rails. Within a couple of years after the opening of the Stockton and Darlington, some investors decided to build a line between Liverpool and Manchester. Stockton and Darlington were relatively small places, remembered today mainly for the historic railway. Liverpool, however, was one of the world's busiest seaports, through which an enormous amount of manufactured goods and raw materials constantly passed. Manchester was one of Great Britain's three major manufacturing centers. So a railway connecting two of the world's most important industrial centers could be extremely lucrative.

The organizers of the Liverpool and Manchester Railway knew that the Stockton and Darlington line had had trouble with its early locomotives. They offered a prize of £500 for whoever built the best locomotive for their line. The contestants were to make ten round-trips over a set distance. Three locomotives were entered, including one built by Stephenson and his son Robert, who would go on to be an important railroad builder. The Stephenson locomotive won with an average speed of 24 miles (38.6 kilometers) per hour. (It could reach 15 miles [24.2 kilometers] per hour when drawing 13 tons [11.8 metric tons].)

One of the most famous of the early engines was George Stephenson's Rocket, a primitive-looking machine that nonetheless outperformed all others of its time. It was built in 1829.

The Liverpool and Manchester had been intended mainly to carry freight, but it had some passenger cars as well. People traveling between these two busy cities quickly realized that they could get from one to the other much faster and more comfortably by train than by a carriage jolting over the bumpy roads of the time. Passenger traffic soon soared, and for a period passengers were bringing in more profits than freight.

A DRAWING MADE IN 1831 OF THE EARLY LIVERPOOL AND MANCHESTER TRAINS. THE ONE ON TOP IS CARRYING FREIGHT, THE BOTTOM ONE LIVESTOCK. BUT IT WAS NOT LONG BEFORE THE OWNERS OF THE LINE LEARNED THAT THEY COULD MAKE SUBSTANTIAL PROFITS CARRYING PASSENGERS, TOO.

To build on this popularity, the operators of the Liverpool and Manchester saw to it that the bridges and stations on their line were well designed and well built. This was during the early Victorian Age. The taste of the time was for grandeur, for buildings and structures covered with a great deal of decoration. Architects looked back to both the Roman empire and the rich Gothic style of medieval churches and castles. When the London and Birmingham Railway, linking England's two other great manufacturing centers, was built a few years after the Liverpool and Manchester, the stations at the terminal cities were even grander than those of the Liverpool and Manchester line, adorned with columns and arches in the Roman manner. These stations were visible evidence that the railroad was an enterprise of great importance. Even today in the

THE FABULOUS ISAMBARD KINGDOM BRUNEL POSES AGAINST A STACK OF LARGE CHAINS. BRUNEL WAS BOTH AN ENGINEER AND A BUSINESSMAN. HE WAS KNOWN FOR HIS DARING AND IMAGINATIVE VENTURES—LIKE THE GREAT EASTERN STEAMSHIPS—AND FOR HIS GREAT WESTERN RAILWAY.

United States we still find many grandiose railways stations in our big cities, like Grand Central Station in New York, with its columns, arches, and star-filled ceiling 100 feet (30.5 meters) above the floor.

The railway system being built in England set the pattern for railways everywhere. In general, there was little overall planning. Lines were set down by whoever wanted to do so wherever they wanted to build them. Each railway company had its own cars and locomotives designed to its own specific taste. Isambard Kingdom Brunel dug a railway tunnel through the rock of Box Hill at a fairly steep angle. It was later discovered that the rising sun shines from end to end of the tunnel each April 9—Brunel's birthday. This was hardly the best reason for how to position a railway tunnel.

Brunel also insisted on using a very wide 7-foot (2.1-meter) gauge, or track width, for his Great Western Railway running from London to Bristol. Until then, gauges had been 4 feet 8.5 inches (1.4 meters) wide. Brunel believed that his 7-foot (2.1-meter) gauge offered passengers a smoother ride.

In 1845 a commission was established to decide on a standard gauge for Great Britain. High-speed trials were set up. Brunel's Great Western locomotive reached 60 miles (96.6 kilometers) per hour hauling 80 tons (72.6 metric tons) on the broad 7-foot (2.1-meter) gauge, while Stephenson trains on the narrower gauge reached only 53 miles (85.3 kilometers) per hour. One railway historian wrote, "Although the Commission considered the 7-foot [2.1-meter] gauge in every way superior," they settled for the narrow gauge simply because most of the tracks in England had already been laid to that width. All over the world it is still being used today.

THIS EARLY AMERICAN RAILWAY TRAIN USED ORDINARY HORSE-DRAWN CARRIAGES FITTED WITH RAILROAD WHEELS FOR ITS PASSENGER CARS. SOON THEREAFTER, PASSENGER CARS SPECIALLY DESIGNED FOR RAILWAYS WERE BEING BUILT.

The Rails Come to America

The rapid development of England's marvelous new system of transportation attracted the attention of the rest of the world. Other nations were industrializing as well, and they saw the great advantages of moving their products and people by rail. The first railway was built in Germany in 1835, in Belgium the same year, and in Italy in 1839. But it was the United States that would go on to develop the largest railway system in the world.

The United States was as large as all of Europe, much of it without roads or even wagon trails. It was also cut by two great mountain chains near the eastern and western ends of the landmass. The vast river system had made water transport possible. But steamboat travel was slow and subject to the whims of the weather. Furthermore, steamboats could go only where there was water of a certain depth: across the vast plains west of the Mississippi there were large spaces without navigable rivers.

Railroads, however, could go anywhere. True, the early locomotives had trouble hauling heavy freight trains up mountains. But the mountains could be tamed by digging tunnels, as Brunel had done. They could also be cut and filled. That is, gorges could be sliced through high points and the earth used to fill in the low points, thus producing a more level trackway. Engineers still use this technique today in building superhighways. An added advantage was that the whole central portion of the United States was relatively flat—ideal land for railways.

Rails were first used in the United States, as they had been in England, for hauling coal and other minerals in horse-drawn carts. In 1827 the Baltimore and Ohio Railroad, using horses, was founded. The next year the Delaware and Hudson Canal Company opened a horse-drawn railway from Honesdale to Carbondale, Pennsylvania. Almost immediately, the company—well aware of railway advances in England—bought two locomotives from an English company. One of these, the Stourbridge Lion, made a trip on August 8, 1829, making it the first steam train to operate in the United States. However, those English locomotives were found to be too heavy for American rails. So Americans began to make their own locomotives. And by the late 1830s, the American industry, with so much land to cover, was booming.

The explosion was, like most explosions, chaotic. Investors were not interested in creating a carefully planned railway system for the new nation, but in making profits, the more the better. Most railroads built in those early years were "short lines," set up to link one city to another community fairly nearby. The country was expanding quickly. Beginning at almost the same moment as the railway boom was the great wave of immigration into the United States, mainly from Europe, but from Asia as well. These newcomers would swell cities, both large and small, and would provide both workers and customers for the rapidly growing industries being created in the United States. City officials and factory owners believed that it was necessary to have rail lines connecting cities to the rest of the nation. There was a building fear that lacking a rail connection, a city would be left behind to wither financially.

The U.S. government also believed that the nation must develop a great railway system if it was to become a world power. The rich farmland of the Midwest needed good systems of transportation to carry its huge yields of wheat, corn, hogs, cattle, and other products to the populous cities of the East and nations abroad. The same was true of the South, with its tobacco and cotton, and of the Northeast, with its textiles.

THE NEW STEAM RAILWAY GENERATED CONSIDERABLE PUBLIC EXCITEMENT. A RACE WAS ARRANGED BETWEEN A HORSE AND THE CELEBRATED ENGINE TOM THUMB ON AUGUST 25, 1830. HORSES COULD USUALLY OUTRUN THESE EARLY STEAM ENGINES FOR BRIEF PERIODS, BUT THEY WOULD SOON TIRE AND LOSE THEIR LEAD.

As a consequence, the national government and cities and towns across America were not merely willing, but eager, to encourage railroad building. Given this attitude on the part of governments large and small, it was hardly surprising that investors leaped in. Thus began one of the greatest industrial scandals in American history. Towns, cities, states, and federal government agencies began handing out huge grants of money and land to hastily assembled railway corporations. Many of the railroads built during these years were badly made and eventually had to be rebuilt by the towns and cities that had so unwisely subsidized them. In other cases, the investors in the railway lines quietly formed their own construction firms, which heavily overbilled the cities for their work. In still other cases, the investors took the subsidies, and the tracks were never laid.

The scandalous corruption could not have occurred had city, state, and federal officials all been honest. Unfortunately, there was so much money to be made in railroad building that there was plenty available for bribes. Railway officials paid mayors, congressmen, and city aldermen millions of dollars to give away land for rail lines and stations, and to hold their noses when the bills came in.

Perhaps the most egregious handouts were to the builders of long-distance lines extending into the Great Plains and beyond to the Pacific coast. In 1848, as a consequence of the Mexican War, the United States claimed the Southwest and California. At around the same time, gold was

THE STEAM RAILWAY WAS VERY IMPORTANT IN THE DEVELOPMENT OF THE AMERICAN WEST. THE FLAT LAND OF THE PLAINS WAS IDEAL FOR LAYING TRACKS. THE TRAINS MOVING THROUGH THE HEARTLAND ALLOWED FARMERS TO SHIP THEIR CROPS EASILY TO THE POPULOUS CITIES OF THE EAST. WITHOUT THE RAILROAD, THE WEST WOULD HAVE BEEN MUCH SLOWER TO DEVELOP.

THE ENTHUSIASM FOR RAILROADS INSPIRED A FAMOUS SERIES OF CURRIER AND IVES PRINTS. THE TWO ARTISTS ISSUED MANY RAILROAD PRINTS, WHICH WERE EAGERLY BOUGHT BY THE PUBLIC. THIS ONE, ENTITLED "WESTWARD THE COURSE OF EMPIRE TAKES ITS WAY," NOT ONLY CELEBRATED THE RAILROADS BUT THE SWELLING AMERICAN PRIDE IN THE SUDDEN GROWTH OF ITS "EMPIRE."

discovered near San Francisco. Interest, too, was growing in the fertile lands of the Pacific Northwest. Newly arrived immigrants and people scratching livings from the worn soil of the East were looking westward. Congress believed that transcontinental lines linking the nation from coast to coast would allow the western territories to fill with people and create general prosperity for the whole country. Railways would carry wheat, corn, and hogs from the farmlands of the West to the cities of the East, and carry back machinery and household goods in return.

In order to encourage railroaders to build such lines, Congress offered them, at no charge, huge sections of the western lands for their tracks. The land was often given in strips 50 miles (80.5 kilometers) wide. Why so large? Obviously, land within a reasonable wagon ride of the railroad line would be worth far more than land some distance away. In this way the railroads came into possession of the most valuable land in the West. Not only would the railroad corporations make money from carrying freight and passengers, they would profit enormously from selling land along their lines, where towns and villages were springing up. Eventually the federal government and various states and cities gave the railroads parcels of land equal in size to Texas.

The result, for better or worse, was a sprawling rail system with tentacles spreading everywhere across the country. In 1830 there were only 23 miles (37 kilometers) of track in the United States; by 1860 there were 30,636 miles (49,303 kilometers). The Civil War, which began in 1861, spurred the growth even more: rail transport was essential for carrying troops and war materials in and out of combat zones. Both sides had to spend money on their railroads. One important reason for the ultimate triumph of the North was its more highly developed industrial machine, which was greatly dependent on rail transportation.

Inevitably, with no overall plan, railroaders used whatever gauge track suited them. This meant that freight and passengers frequently had to be unloaded in one city and loaded onto another train with the right gauge in order to continue their journey. This inefficiency was not tolerable during the Civil War, when the rapid transit of supplies and men was essential, and pressure for a uniform gauge increased. After many negotiations, the railroads settled on the standard 4 feet 8.5 inches (1.4 meters) used in England, for the same reason—that it was already the most widely used.

The railroads were also responsible for another innovation. Under the preindustrial system, when travel was slow and it might take weeks to move by sailing ship or stage coach 1,000 miles (1,610 kilometers), the differences in timekeeping from place to place did not really matter. As a consequence, towns only a dozen miles apart might run on somewhat different time systems: it might be twelve-thirty in one town when it was one o'clock in another one nearby.

The coming of the railroads suddenly made a standard time system necessary. While each area was still setting its own time, a train leaving Centerville at noon might reach West Centerville at 11:45 a.m. Sched-

This photograph shows the celebrated moment when a golden spike was driven in 1869, finally joining the railroad lines that had been built from opposite directions, the east and west. Politicians and celebrities of the day attended the event.

ules proved almost impossible to work out. Worse, confusion about where a train was supposed to be at a given moment might lead to two trains arriving at the same place simultaneously, often with disastrous results. In 1847 the British government passed a law requiring all British railroads to operate on Greenwich Mean Time, the international standard now in use. Inevitably, English towns discovered that they could not use a time system different from the one the railroads were using, and Greenwich Mean Time was quickly adopted across England.

The United States had a more complicated problem: when it was breakfast time in California, it was lunchtime in Rhode Island. Americans struggled with this problem for several years. Finally, in 1883, a conference was called resulting in the country's being divided into the four time zones we use today—Eastern, Central, Mountain, and Pacific. The steam revolution had even changed the nature of time itself.

By the end of the Civil War, the American railway system had matured. But it continued to grow, the network of tracks eventually spreading deeper into the West. In 1862 plans were laid for a cross-country rail line. The Union Pacific would build westward from the Missouri River, the Central Pacific eastward from Sacramento, California. In May 1869 the two lines met at Promontory, west of Ogden, Utah. A golden spike was driven to mark the event, and the nation was now joined by rails.

An important innovation of the time was the invention of the air brake by George Westinghouse. He was born in a little town in upstate New York, where his father had a small machine shop. He was entranced with machinery as a boy. When he was only nineteen, he took out a patent on his first invention, a small steam engine. At twenty he happened to see a train derailment, a common enough occurrence in those days, given the shoddy roadbeds that had been laid by corrupt railroad corporations. Westinghouse watched the workmen struggle to get the cars back on the tracks. He went home determined to devise a better way of putting railroad cars back on their tracks. It took him some time to find backing for his "car replacer," but eventually he did. It worked, and his career as an inventor began.

While still young, he was riding in a train which was held up because of a collision between two trains farther down the line. The engineers of the colliding trains had seen each other while they were still some distance apart and had blown their whistles. At the time, brakes could not be controlled from the engine cab, but had to be screwed down individually on each car by a brakeman. In this case, the brakemen had not been able to stop the trains in time.

Westinghouse realized that a better braking system would save both lives and money, and earn him considerable profits, as well. He knew about some French engineers who were using air-pressure drills to bore tunnels through mountains. Westinghouse saw immediately that air pressure was the answer to the braking problem. Again he had trouble getting financing, but eventually he found the money he needed, and his new system was installed on a test train. It had barely left the station when it came upon a wagon stuck on the railroad track. The engineer grabbed the handle of the new air brakes and stopped the train 4 feet (1.2 meters) from the wagon. Using the old system, the train could not have been stopped before smashing into the wagon. The value of Westinghouse's air brakes was quickly proved, and Westinghouse went on to found the huge corporation still operating today.

Air brakes dramatically increased the safety of railroading. At the same time, roadbeds were being improved and tracks made more secure. Taking a train was no longer an adventure, but a regular part of human life—not only in Europe and America, but increasingly so elsewhere in the world.

With safety improved, the focus then shifted to passenger comfort. In Europe, there were usually three classes of passenger cars. First-class passengers rode in individual compartments that might seat up to six people. They featured comfortable upholstered seats, carpeting, and

WITH MANY RAILROAD LINES OPERATING ON SINGLE TRACKS, COLLISIONS WERE INEVITABLE. HERE, ONE ENGINE ENDED UP ON TOP OF ANOTHER. THE INTRODUCTION OF THE WESTINGHOUSE AIR BRAKE REDUCED THE NUMBER OF ACCIDENTS, BUT MISHAPS STILL OCCURRED.

AMERICANS SOMETIMES SPENT SEVERAL DAYS ON A TRAIN TRIP. TO MAKE THE TRIP
MORE COMFORTABLE, WELL-APPOINTED DINING AND PARLOR CARS WERE ADDED.
THIS ADVERTISEMENT SHOWS A DINING CAR WITH A WAITER TAKING ORDERS.

generous spaces for stowing luggage. Many had dining cars attached, where uniformed waiters served hot meals. Third-class passengers sat on rows of benches and ate the food they had brought from home. Second-class passengers got something in between. Of course, first-class service cost a great deal more than the others.

In the United States, which prided itself on being democratic, there was a tendency to shy away from this passenger class system. Nonetheless, some passenger cars were opulent, with crystal chandeliers, upholstered seats, curtains on the windows, carpets, and even vases of flowers. Given the size of America, passengers often spent several days on a train. Various sorts of parlor, club, and bar cars were provided where passengers could gossip, play cards, and drink.

The most famous of these luxurious cars were the Pullmans. George Pullman was born in 1831 just as the railroads were starting their great rise in America. He worked first as a cabinetmaker. In 1859, living in Chicago, he began to remodel old passenger cars into luxurious ones. In the mid-1860s he went a step further and built the first sleeper cars. They had seats that converted into beds, much as they do today—especially in Europe where the *couchette* is still widely used. Pullman did not sell his cars,

A SLEEPING CAR, PROBABLY FROM THE 1920S. AT THE TIME, PULLMANS SUCH AS THIS ONE WERE THE GLAMOROUS WAY TO TRAVEL LONG DISTANCES.

but rented them to the railroads. The Pullman cars became something of a national institution. In particular, Pullman porters were almost always African American. These men had polished manners, handsome uniforms, and traveled widely; they were much admired in the African-American community of the day.

By the second half of the nineteenth century, railways were spreading around the world. In 1853 a 21-mile (33.8-kilometer) stretch of railway was opened between Bombay and Thāne, in India. China got its first railway in 1876, a 5-mile (8-kilometer) stretch between Shanghai and Wusong. Service opened in Malaya in 1885 with a line between Taiping and Port Weld. Australia got a railway in 1854, a 13-mile (21-kilometer) stretch between Melbourne and Hobson's Bay. South Africa started its first public railway in 1861, a 2-mile (3.2-kilometer) line between Durban and the Point. By the late 1800s, there were railways practically everywhere in the world.

The effect on human life, especially in the industrialized world, was profound. In the United States, the linking of the Atlantic and Pacific coasts by rail opened the way for the development of the West Coast, which today is both prosperous and populous. The move west was no longer a fateful decision, involving a terrible trek across plains and deserts; it was easy to visit the West and come back east if things didn't work out.

A more subtle effect of the railroads happened in the 1870s and 1880s. In the East, there were many railroad lines, sometimes three or more serving a single city. Shippers could pick the line with the cheapest rates, so prices were kept in check by competition. On the Great Plains, settled by farmers hacking hard livings out of the soil, most areas were served by a single line. Railroads there usually held monopolies and began charging the farmers such high rates for shipping their wheat and other products that the farmers could not make a profit. It was the railroads, not the farmers, that were reaping the benefits.

The farmers retaliated, organizing themselves into activist groups, the best known of which was the Grange. They managed to get laws passed in several states controlling the prices of railroad freight. Eventually the Supreme Court struck down these laws as unconstitutional: railroads were engaged in interstate commerce, and only the federal government could regulate interstate commerce.

The railroads clearly had money, power, and a lot of influence with Congress. But the plight of the farmers was parlous, and the unfair-

THIS CARTOON SHOWS A FARMER BATTLING THE RAILROADS. THE SNAKELIKE RAILROAD HAS ITS COILS WRAPPED AROUND THE U.S. CAPITOL. THERE IS NO DOUBT THAT RAILROAD OFFICIALS BRIBED MANY CONGRESSMEN IN THEIR CRUDE ATTEMPTS TO VICTIMIZE THE FARMERS.

ness so clear, that in 1887 Congress passed the Interstate Commerce Act, which prohibited certain unfair practices the railroads had engaged in. The Interstate Commerce Act was not terribly strong at first, but it was a landmark event. It made it clear that the federal government had a right to regulate private property when it crossed state lines and when the public interest was involved. Today we take it for granted that not only the federal but state governments can set minimum wages, legislate health and safety regulations that businesses must follow, require corporations to label products accurately, and control pollution. That is, governments can, and often must, control private business for the good of its workers, customers, and the general public. This policy began with the effort to keep the railroads from overcharging American farmers.

A perhaps even more significant movement started by the railroads was the creation of the suburbs, not just in America, but in Europe and elsewhere. By the 1870s and 1880s, big industrial cities like Chicago, London, and Berlin were becoming in many ways unpleasant places to live in. Workers in the factories typically earned low wages. Many lived in unsanitary conditions, often with a whole family crowded into two rooms. Poverty created crime, and overcrowding helped to spread disease. People who could afford it, mostly the middle class, wanted to escape the city. Streetcar lines spreading into the city outskirts allowed the middle class to find more living space within an easy commute to the city. Soon the borders of cities began to fill with houses.

The spread of the railroads in several directions from the cities gave suburbanization a second push. Middle-class families found that they could build large, pleasant homes amid grass and trees within less than an hour's train ride to the city. The father could commute to his job downtown, while the mother and children remained in their ordered, spacious community. The greatest suburban boom would come later, with the rise of the automobile, but it was a movement triggered by the railroads.

The move to the suburbs caused substantial changes in people's lives. Fathers had less time to work and play alongside their children than they did on farms and in city neighborhoods. Many became distant figures who disappeared early in the morning and reappeared at dinnertime. Children spent more time playing with their friends or involved in activities outside the home. Some families began to splinter. Steam, thus, eventually altered the social fabric of America.

STEAM CARS AND STEAM BUSES GREW IN POPULARITY IN THE CLOSING DECADES OF THE 1800S. THEY WERE POWERFUL AND COULD CARRY LARGER LOADS THAN THE GASOLINE-POWERED AUTOMOBILES THAT WERE BEING DEVELOPED AT THE TIME. HERE, AN AMERICAN STEAM BUS FROM ABOUT 1880.

The End of the Age of Steam

Railroads were not the only means of transportation that were using steam. In the early 1800s, Cugnot, Trevithick, and others, had built rudimentary steam carriages. That type of steam vehicle showed great promise, and under different circumstances efficient steam-driven cars could have been developed. However, the railroads proved to be a better transportation system, given the inadequate roads of the day, and the steam car did not become popular.

By the 1870s, however, the internal-combustion engine was being worked out, and some people turned their attention back to the idea of the steam-driven car as a possible alternative to a gas-operated one. Some steam buses were built. They were cumbersome but very powerful. In 1878 a steam bus was in operation that could run 26 miles (41.9 kilometers) per hour carrying sixteen people. Another one weighed 28 tons (25.4 metric tons) and could carry 100 tons (90.7 metric tons) of people and freight.

Quickly inventors began designing steam automobiles meant to be used by individual drivers. Many of these proved to be effective, powerful, and fast. The first automobile race, run from Paris to Rouen, was won by a steamer, or steam-driven car, which averaged 11.6 miles (18.7 kilometers) per hour over a 79-mile (127.2-kilometer) course. In fact, around 1900, in America steamers and electric cars were more popular

BY THE TWENTIETH CENTURY, RAILROADS HAD BECOME THE PRIMARY MEANS OF TRANSPORTING BOTH PASSENGERS AND FREIGHT. WITHOUT STEAM RAILWAYS, THE INDUSTRIAL SYSTEM COULD NOT HAVE DEVELOPED AS IT DID. IN THIS PICTURE, TRAINS OVERLAP AND CRISSCROSS IN A BUSY SECTION OF RICHMOND, VIRGINIA.

than cars powered by internal-combustion gasoline engines. Perhaps the most famous of them all were the Stanley Steamers. These were fast, reliable, and powerful, and there were a fair number of them still on the road in the 1920s.

But a steamer had drawbacks: you had to build up a head of steam before one could be driven, and there was a limit to how far it could go before you had to take on more fuel and water. In the end, gasoline-powered cars took over.

But steam remained paramount on the rails. One authority says, "The first half of the twentieth century may truly be called the Golden Age of railways. The railway was the primary form of transportation for moving people and freight."

The railroads were essential: without them to carry coal to factories, iron ore to steel mills, steel to factories, and the goods pouring out of those factories into the shops and stores of the world, the industrial system would have foundered. And, of course, tens of millions of people were now dependent on trains to carry them to and from their jobs.

This was less true of the undeveloped nations of Asia, Africa, and elsewhere. In such places tens of millions of people continued to live in villages and small towns, mainly farming, but also practicing traditional handicrafts like weaving and making pots and cookware by hand. Nonetheless, even these people were affected by the steam locomotive. As the world became increasingly interconnected, the manufactured goods that people in nonindustrial countries increasingly bought and the raw materials they sold ultimately had to travel by steam railroads and steamships.

In the developed world, the movement was generally toward bigger and better. The more cars an engine could haul, the lower the freight charges. Longer trains needed larger engines, so everything grew accordingly. Schoolchildren of the day stood at railroad crossings counting the cars on great trains as they lumbered by; a train with a hundred cars was, by the 1930s, no novelty. These trains needed huge locomotives.

In 1922 England saw the introduction of the A1 Pacific, the biggest locomotive in general use in that country. One of those engines achieved the world record for steam in 1938, with a speed of 126 miles (202.9 kilometers) per hour. The Pacifics were hailed and sold around the world.

The Pacific models were popular in the United States, too, and were widely used for high-speed passenger trains. For passengers, especially on long-distance trips, like the run from Chicago to Saint Louis, or New York to Miami, speed was critically important. Before 1935, airplane passenger service was still in its infancy. An air trip was a novelty, and it was not until after World War II that flying become commonplace for large numbers of people.

In the United States, a certain aura of romance was attached to the celebrated passenger trains, like the Southern Pacific's Sunset Limited or the Pennsylvania Railroad's Broadway Limited. The most celebrated of them all was the Twentieth Century Limited, which was used by travelers going between the east and west coasts. Such trains often carried movie stars to and from Hollywood. Stars arriving on the Twentieth Century Limited were often met at New York's Grand Central Terminal by photographers and were ushered off the train onto red carpets rolled over on the platform for the occasion. Trains like the Twentieth Century Limited were sometimes featured on radio shows and in movies as symbols of the rich and glamorous life supposedly lived by the people who traveled on them. Passengers had private compartments with their own bathrooms and were attended by uniformed porters who could be summoned to bring food and drink.

The glamour quotient was increased in the 1930s by the vogue for streamlining. The idea was to sheath locomotives in carefully shaped coverings meant to reduce air resistance. In 1936 the Pennsylvania Railroad hired a famous industrial designer, Raymond Loewy, to dress up some of their locomotives. It is doubtful that streamlining did much to improve the efficiency of these trains, but their shapely forms gave them a stylishly modern look.

But even as steam was reaching its peak in power, glamour, and importance, the seeds of its demise were being sowed. During the nine-

THE TWENTIETH CENTURY LIMITED WAS THE MOST GLAMOROUS OF ALL AMERICAN TRAINS. HERE, WELL-TO-DO TRAVELERS DINE IN COMFORT AS THE TRAIN SPEEDS THROUGH THE COUNTRYSIDE. THE PICTURE WAS TAKEN IN 1948. ALTHOUGH AIR TRAVEL WAS RAPIDLY INCREASING, MOST LONG-DISTANCE TRAVEL WAS STILL CONDUCTED BY TRAIN.

teenth century, many scientists were struggling to turn a strange force, electricity, into a useful source of power. In 1849 the first dynamo was built, and in 1882 Thomas Alva Edison installed the first electrical power system in a section of New York City. The development of electric power was astonishingly fast. Soon the horse-drawn cars that had provided much of the transportation around cities were electrified. Electricity also made it possible to run what came to be called subways underground. The coal smoke and water vapor produced by steam engines would have been intolerable in tunnels, making the air unbreathable after a few trains had passed through. Electric power was the answer. London's subway opened in 1890, Boston's in 1897, while the New York City system began operating in 1904. Other cities soon followed.

Inevitably, railway companies began to electrify their trains. The first electric locomotives in the United States were installed by the Baltimore and Ohio Railroad in 1895. By the 1930s major American railroads, like the Pennsylvania Railroad and the New York Central, were electrifying portions of their lines. The Milwaukee Road put in overhead electric lines on its railways through the mountains of Montana, Idaho, and Washington. Electricity was found to be also particularly useful for short commuter lines: the New Haven electrified its Connecticut commuter line, which carried huge numbers of people into New York City every day.

An even greater threat to steam was the new diesel system. In 1890 a German engineer named Rudolf Diesel conceived the idea of a new type of internal-combustion engine that challenged the only recently invented gasoline engine. In the diesel system, the mixture of fuel and air was compressed so highly that it ignited spontaneously. It was a simpler system and could run on cheaper, lower-grade fuel. Diesel patented his invention in 1892 and within a few years had an operating model. Diesel engines quickly proved to be especially practical for heavy-duty work and today are still in use in tractor trailers and most large trucks.

By 1925 diesel locomotives were being used in rail yards for switching. In 1934 the Budd Company built its Pioneer Zephyr for passengers, and so-called Budd cars are still used today on many rail lines. Then, in

STREAMLINING WAS INTRODUCED IN THE 1930S. THE NEW, SLEEK SHAPE OF LOCOMOTIVES ADDED BEAUTY AND APPEAL BUT HAD LITTLE PRACTICAL VALUE.

By the 1930s, commuters were increasingly driving themselves to work, rather than taking trains. The heyday of the railroad would soon be over.

1939, General Motors produced a powerful diesel locomotive for use in freight service. It quickly showed that it could do almost anything better than steam engines. The transition to diesel was temporarily stopped by World War II, when men and materials to build a new fleet of locomotives were not available. But with the end of the war in 1945, the transition to diesel was rapid. By the mid-1950s, many railroads had replaced their steam engines with diesels.

It was not just new types of engines that were driving steam engines into retirement; there were new types of transportation competing with railways and steamships, too. For one, the automobile—which boomed in America in the 1920s and in Europe after World War II—began drawing passengers away from railroads. Millions of people began commuting to work by car, rather than by train. They also started using their cars instead of trains for vacations, business trips, and jaunts to see friends and relatives in neighboring cities.

The rapid proliferation of automobiles brought an outcry for better roads. New interstate routes, parkways, and superhighways made it possible for trucks to carry freight from city to city, going directly from the factory loading dock to stores without any reloading. The railways lost a huge amount of freight business to truck lines.

Then, as air travel became cheaper after World War II—especially with the development of jets—people began to fly from Los Angeles to Chicago, from Boston to London. Long-distance passenger trains suffered; so did the great steamship lines like Cunard. Even in the 1950s, most vacationers took ships from the Americas to Europe or Asia. But by the 1960s, most long-distance travel was by plane, and the steam locomotive had all but vanished in the United States.

It lasted only slightly longer elsewhere. In England, steam continued to be in use until 1968, and it lingered in other places as steam engines remained in service until they wore out. Today nearly all railroads run on either electric or diesel power or, in many cases, both.

Steam engines did stay in use for a while in ships. For one thing, although in time electrically powered boats were devised, in general large ships could not be run by electric engines: ships could not be "plugged in" to an electrical system as subway trains could, and electric power on such a big scale was difficult to produce onboard. But diesel engines were easily adapted to ships, and in time the steamship went the way of the steam locomotive.

Surprisingly, it was not the end of the age of steam. That story begins, as so many stories do, with the ancient Greeks. In about 100 C.E., Hero of Alexandria invented a device in which two pipes, bent at angles, released steam from a globe, which was then set spinning on an axle. Hero had no way of knowing that his little plaything was demonstrating a crucially important law proclaimed by Isaac Newton fifteen centuries later: every action has an equal and opposite reaction. For example, when you fire a rifle, the bullet will be shot forward. At the same time, the rifle will be "shot" backward against your shoulder. This is the principle on which the jet plane works: when hot gas of some type is spewed out of the rear of the jet engine, the plane is at the same time shoved forward in an equal but opposite reaction.

Unfortunately, Hero's idea was ignored for a long time. Not until the 1800s did anyone exploit the principle to produce what came to be called the turbine engine.

The first turbine engines were actually based on a different principle. The waterwheel, in which a stream of water pushes the blades of a large wheel around, had been in use for a long time. Eventually the water turbine emerged, in which a stream of rapidly plummeting water, as in Niagara Falls, drops onto the blades within the turbine, causing them to revolve rapidly. These turbines are called impulse turbines. They are widely used today in hydroelectric plants—water-driven electricity-generating systems.

Another type of turbine, based on the old Hero idea, was worked out shortly after the impulse turbine. As electricity became practical in the

A NINETEENTH-CENTURY STEAM ENGINE INTENDED FOR USE ON A SHIP. STEAM CONTINUED TO POWER SHIPS INTO THE 1960S, BUT IN THE END DIESEL TOOK OVER.

TURBINES ARE STILL IMPORTANT FOR GENERATING THE MASSIVE AMOUNT OF ELECTRICITY MODERN SOCIETY REQUIRES. SOME ARE RUN BY THE FORCE OF FALLING WATER, SUCH AS NIAGARA FALLS. OTHERS ARE POWERED BY STEAM.

second half of the nineteenth century, it was realized that generators needed to spin at very high speeds, at least 1,200 revolutions per minute. Charles Algernon Parsons, the son of a British aristocrat, was one of the first to work out a reaction turbine, based on the jet principle. In such turbines a jet of steam is shot from a nozzle in each turbine blade. In reaction, the blades are pushed back in the opposite direction, making them spin around their axle. Parsons developed a special dynamo to accompany his turbine. It could generate 7.5 kilowatts at 100 volts revolving 18,000 times a minute. The steam turbine engine was first used in an English ship, the *Turbina,* which set a speed record of 34.5 knots (63.9 kilometers per hour) in 1897. Turbines increasingly took over from the old reciprocating engine In 1888 a turbine was installed in a public power station in Newcastle, England. By the turn of the century, turbines were being used in the famous ocean liners *Mauritania* and *Lusitania* of the Cunard Line. By 1920 oil, instead of coal, was being used to fuel steam turbines. The *Queen Mary,* quite possibly the most famous of all the ocean liners of the time, used steam turbines, as did the *Q.E. II.* Steam turbines were still being installed on large, fast ships as late as the 1960s, but in general, steam could no longer compete with diesel engines.

Today steam turbines are used in a wide range of industries, in machines that make and process pulp and paper, textiles, and food. They are, says one authority, "the most efficient way to generate electricity. Commercial systems all use turbines." Some of these, of course, are water-driven turbines, like the ones powered by Niagara Falls. Nonetheless, about 15 percent of American energy consumption goes toward making steam for industry.

Surprisingly, that percentage may actually increase. In general, nuclear power plants work by generating steam: the energy given off in the process of nuclear fission is used to turn water into steam, which is then employed to drive turbines to produce electricity.

HERE, A WORKER ASSEMBLES A STEAM TURBINE. ALTHOUGH STEAM ENGINES ARE NO LONGER AT THE HEART OF THE INDUSTRIAL SYSTEM, STEAM CONTINUES TO PLAY AN IMPORTANT ROLE IN THE WORLD ECONOMY.

Modern steam turbines are of course far more sophisticated than the old reciprocating beam engines of Newcomen and Watt. They use steam that is heated to very high temperatures at great pressure, all of which requires complex technology. But it is steam, nonetheless, the same stuff that made the Industrial Revolution possible and so drastically changed the world we live in. Steam is with us still and will undoubtedly be with us for some time to come.

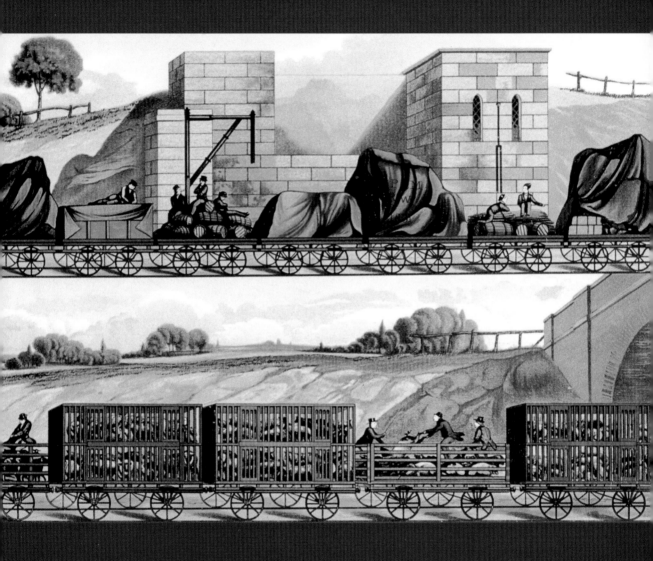

air brake—A device to reduce speed and operated by compressed air.

atmospheric pressure—The pressure on the earth's surface caused by the weight of the air in the atmosphere.

axle—A shaft on which a wheel rotates.

colliery—Another term for a coal mine, generally including all the buildings and machines on the surface.

condenser—A device designed to cool the exhaust steam from a turbine to below the boiling point so that it can be returned to the heat source as water.

cross tie—A beam supporting and connecting rails or train tracks; also known as a *sleeper.*

cylinder—A round hole inside an engine block that provides space for the movement of a piston.

langed—Having a ridge or projection used for stability and guiding movement along a track.

flywheel—A rotating device used to minimize fluctuations in velocity.

gauge—The distance between the rails of a train track.

hopper—A freight car with a door in the floor through which materials are unloaded.

impulse turbine—A rotary engine driven by a stream of usually liquid directly contacting a revolving system of blades.

internal-combustion engine—A system in which fuel is burned within the engine in order to generate power.

lever—A simple machine that increases power usually consisting of a simple bar pivoting on a fulcrum.

monopoly—The state in which a single company owns all or nearly all of the means of production and distribution for a given product or service.

piston—A short solid piece of metal that moves up and down inside the cylinder of an engine in order to press the fuel into a small space and to send the power produced by it to the wheels.

pulley—A simple machine used for lifting and consisting of a wheel with a grooved rim in which a length of cord or chain is threaded. looped around a support, usually a grooved wheel.

rack and pinion—A device used to convert motion in which a gear engages a toothed rod to achieve, usually, the rotation of wheels.

reaction turbine—An engine that generates rotation through the equal and opposite reaction of the blade to jets of steam.

reciprocating engine—An internal-combustion engine in which a crankshaft is turned by pistons moving up and down in cylinders.

vacuum—A space in which the pressure is significantly lower than the atmospheric pressure.

valve—A device that is used to control the flow of a substance, usually water or air.

winch—A lifting device consisting of a horizontal cylinder turned by a crank on which a cable or rope winds.

Time Line

1606
Giambattista della Porta develops a device that uses steam to force water along a pipe.

1654
German inventor Otto von Guericke develops an air pump able to create vacuums.

around 1680
Samuel Morland designs a steam-driven machine that is able to raise and lower a piston in a cylinder.

early 1690s
French inventor Denis Papin produces a vacuum using steam but does not develop the idea.

1699
Thomas Savery demonstrates a steam-powered water pump.

by 1712
Thomas Newcomen develops the first working steam engine.

1770
Nicolas-Joseph Cugnot successfully tests his steam tractor.

1776
James Watt and Matthew Boulton begin operating their new steam engines at the Bloomfield Colliery.

1779–1787
James Watt, Matthew Wasborough, James Picard, and others introduce a series of innovations to steam-powered land vehicles including the addition of a crank, a flywheel, and improvements to the suspension, engine, and gears.

1787
John Fitch's steam-powered boat successfully operates on the Delaware River. James Rumsey's model is demonstrated on the Potomac River.

1798
Richard Trevithick begins work on his engine in which the piston is powered directly by steam and not atmospheric pressure.

1803
The paddle wheeler *Charlotte Dundas* is launched in Scotland.
Richard Trevithick successfully drives his steam carriage around London.

1804
Richard Trevithick's railway successfully operates at Pen-y-darren.

1807

Robert Fulton's *Clermont* becomes the first steamship to offer regular passenger service in the United States.

1812

Richard Trevithick develops a threshing machine.

1819

The *Savannah* completes the first successful transatlantic crossing powered entirely by steam.

1820s

Jacob Perkins demonstrates a steam-powered machine gun for the Duke of Wellington.

1825

The first public railway to use steam locomotives, the Stockton and Darlington Railway, begins service.

1827

The Baltimore and Ohio railway line opens.

1829

The Stourbridge Lion becomes the first steam train to operate in the United States.

1838

The Great Western Railway opens.

1843

The *Great Britain* is launched, the first transatlantic liner to employ a screw propeller.

1860
More than 30,000 miles (48,280 kilometers) of track have been laid in the United States.

1869
The transcontinental railroad is completed, culminating in the driving of the golden spike at Promontory, Utah.

1892
Rudolf Diesel patents his new fuel system.

1895
America's first electric locomotives are installed by the Baltimore and Ohio Railroad.

1960s
The last steam trains are taken out of regular service in England.

Web Sites

http://inventors.about.com/library/inventors/blsteamengine.htm
This site offers biographies of the key inventors James Savery, Thomas Newcomen, and James Watt as well as links to articles on steamboats, steam turbines, the steam traction engine, and an explanation of how steam engines work.

http://www.history.rochester.edu/steam/
For a more advanced student, the Steam Engine Library offers links to a wealth of historical documents and primary sources related to the history and development of this pivotal invention.

http://www.ideafinder.com/history/inventors/watt.htm
This article, part of the site The Great Idea Finder, offers detailed information and fascinating facts about the life of inventor James Watt.

http://www.geocities.com/Athens/Acropolis/6914/
An invaluable resource, "this site consists of 48 pages concerning the men and the events which led to the steam engine invention."

http://www.egr.msu.edu/~lira/supp/steam/
This site includes, among other things, detailed diagrams and illustrations of Watt's and Newcomen's early models.

http://travel.howstuffworks.com/steam.htm
From How Stuff Works, this page offers links to detailed explanations of the inner workings of steam engines and boilers.

http://americanhistory.si.edu/youmus/ex26rrha.htm
A companion page to the exhibit Railroad Hall, part of the Smithsonian Institution's National Museum of American History. The actual exhibit features classic American locomotives dating from the 1850s to the 1920s.

http://inventors.about.com/library/inventors/blsteamship.htm
This site offers a look at the contributions of Robert Fulton and John Fitch to the glorious age of the steamboat.

Bibliography

Blumberg, Rhoda. *Full Steam Ahead: The Race to Build a Transcontinental Railroad.* Washington, DC: National Geographic, 1996.

Flammang, James M. *Robert Fulton: Inventor and Steamboat Builder.* Historical American Biographies series. Berkeley Heights, NJ: Enslow, 1999.

Greenawald, G. Dale. *The Railroad Era: Business Competition and the Public Interest.* Public Issues series. Boulder, CO: Social Science Education Consortium, 1991.

McCall, Edith. *Mississippi Steamboatmen: The Story of Henry Miller Shreve.* New York: Walker, 1986.

McKissack, Patricia. *A Long Hard Journey: The Story of the Pullman Porter.* New York: Walker, 1995.

Siegel, Beatrice. *The Steam Engine.* Inventions That Changed Our Lives series. New York: Walker, 1986.

Spangenburg, Ray, and Diane Moser. *The Story of America's Railroads.* Connecting a Continent series. New York: Facts on File, 1991.

Stein, R. Conrad. *The Transcontinental Railroad in American History.* In American History series. Berkeley Heights, NJ: Enslow, 1997.

Wormser, Richard L. *The Iron Horse: How Railroads Changed America.* New York: Walker, 1993.

Index

Page numbers for illustrations are in **boldface**.

About the Author

James Lincoln Collier has written books for both adults and students on many subjects, among them the prizewinning novel *My Brother Sam Is Dead.* Many of these books, both fiction and nonfiction, have historical themes, including the highly acclaimed Marshall Cavendish Benchmark series the Drama of American History, which he wrote with Christopher Collier.